T0380768

JUST IMAGINE...

WRITTEN AND ILLUSTRATED
BY

SIMONE SHEPPARD

To order additional copies of this book, contact:
Xlibris
1-888-795-4274
www.Xlibris.com
Orders@Xlibris.com

This book is dedicated to my glorious home planet, Earth.

Imagine, you've been working hard
vacation time has come.
"Let's go camping!" someone says
"That's fun for everyone."
So, off you go, you load the car
with blankets, tent and food.

The weather's hot, the forest's dry,
so fires will be taboo.

Your food is in the cooler, wrapped up well
and locked up tight.

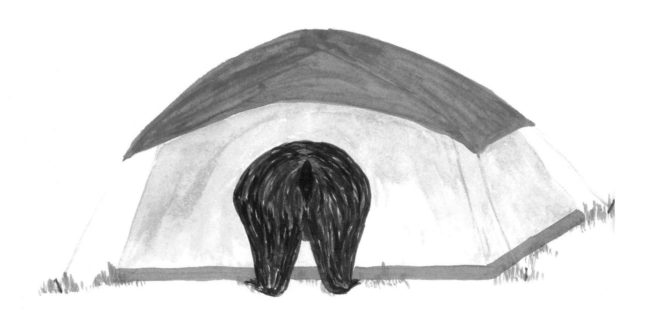

Don't want a visit from a bear
in the middle of the night!

Imagine you're that big black bear
and you live in those woods.
You really don't like people so
you hope that they'll be good.
You hope they won't light matches
and you hope they won't hurt trees
and you hope they take home all their trash
and leave the forest neat.

The food folks bring is tasty
    and perhaps they'll leave you some
but you'd rather have some berries or
    a fresh made honeycomb.

Imagine! You're a honey bee!

And all day long you get to see

inside the prettiest of flowers

which call to you with perfume sweet,

because they know you have the powers
to bring them pollen which they need…

to start to turn themselves to seed

so life can start anew.

And now imagine
you're the flower.
    Just weeks ago
you were so small.
Who would have thought
that sun and water
    could have made
you grow so tall?
But here you are
in all your glory
    waiting for the honey bee,

or maybe hummingbirds will come

and sip your nectar,

gratefully.

Imagine you're that hummingbird

or any bird you want!

You like to swim? Then be a duck

           or sleek black cormorant.

If music is the art you love,

the robin's song is pretty.

Like dressing up? Well…

Parrots come in great variety!

In any case, you'll get to fly

among the trees, up in the sky.

Imagine, you're an old oak tree,

standing where an acorn fell.

For years and years you just get taller.

Just how tall, no-one can tell.

Feeding squirrels, birds and chipmunks

with your acorns every fall.

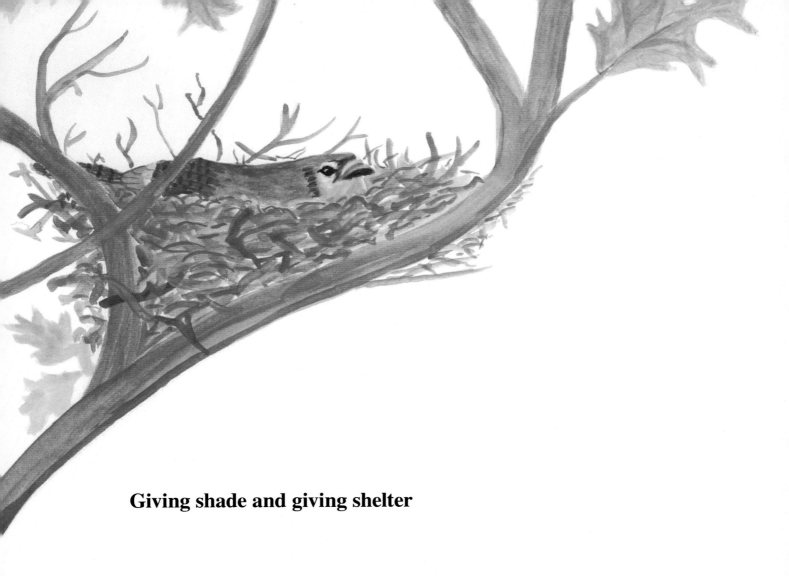

Giving shade and giving shelter

when these creatures come to call.

Perhaps the desert's more your style.

Would you a cactus like to be?

You'll need so little with your very

prickly personality!

Imagine though, you'd still have friends…

a scorpion or two,

perhaps a snake,

a lizard yet,

coyote and tortoise, too.

Most desert life comes out at night.

It's really quite amazing.

It's cooler then for them to feed.

Imagine them star-gazing.

And so at last imagine

    that you are now a star,

way out in the black night sky

    so far away… so far.

You're looking back upon the earth

    so sweet to see again…

Bright with color,

    rich with life,

    a perfect little gem.

Somewhere out behind you

there may be another planet

where things can grow and live and love.

Perhaps one day we'll find it.

But now it's time to come back down

to earth where you belong.

Go out and play, work hard and learn,

laugh, dance and sing your songs.

Enjoy the world around you,

treasure it and do you know what?

If we take care of planet Earth,

Earth will nurture us -

Just imagine that!

This is where we usually write
The End
but I hope this is just
the beginning.